Your Castle Keep

Mado's Lullaby

Michael Piersol

Copyright

Dedication

Dedicated to my loving wife Jamie and our daughter Madeleine, who was the inspiration for this project.

Acknowledgments

Lauren Kidd, who created such wonderful illustrations for this book.

About the Author:

Michael is a school counselor in Reading PA. He lives in Wyomissing PA with his wife, Jamie, and his daughter, Madeleine. He loves to cycle and do weightlifting. He also loves to travel with his family and cook. His favorite destination is France and Ocean City, NJ.

The night arrives too soon for us,
We have so much to say,
We snuggle close, lying still,
As daylight slips away.

Evening will not let us go
And you resist its charms,
I weave a tale of long ago,
as you rest within my arms.

I tell the tale of Knights so bold,
And princesses so fair.
And I sing a little song
As I gently stroke your hair.

I will be your castle keep
Our Princess Fleur de lis
Come rest within my humble walls
Where dreams will never cease.

Just remember, little one,
the world can be unkind.
And when it is, and you are sad,
This song will come to mind.

I will be your castle keep
Our princess fleur de lis,
Come rest within my humble walls
Where dreams will never cease.

Our little one, our petite fleur
May all your dreams come true.
As our dream, some years ago,
Came true when we had you.

Someday you'll have your own to hold.
The sweetest days you'll know.
In each moment that you share,
Sweet memories they'll bestow

Share the memories that you have,
of days when you were small,
The imaginings and reveries
And all that you recall

Perhaps when yours are feeling scared,
And your comfort to them bring.
You may recall the words you learned
And this is what you'll sing.

I will be your castle keep
My princess fleur de lis
Come rest within my humble walls
Where dreams will never cease.

www.ingramcontent.com/pod-product-compliance
Lightning Source LLC
Chambersburg PA
CBHW040906120626
46551CB00006B/668